Short Walks in the

Lake Distr...

**12 Scenic Wa ... ...ing Height
and Lengt. ...suit all Ages**

An Essential Guide for Walking
in the Lake District

Brian Smailes

Nunquam solivagus

THE YORKSHIRE DALES TOP TEN
ISBN 0-9526900-5-5

THE DERBYSHIRE TOP TEN
ISBN 1-903568-03-X

THE COMPLETE ISLE OF WIGHT COASTAL FOOTPATH
ISBN 0-9526900-6-3

ISLE OF WIGHT, NORTH TO SOUTH - EAST TO WEST
ISBN1-903568-07-2

THE NATIONAL 3 PEAKS WALK
ISBN 0-9526900-7-1

THE SCOTTISH COAST TO COAST WALK
ISBN 0-9526900-8-X

17 WALKS IN GLEN NEVIS
ISBN1-903568-05-6

THE GREAT GLEN WAY
ISBN 1-903568-13-7

THE YORKSHIRE 3 PEAKS WALK
ISBN 1-903568-01-3

THE LANCASHIRE TRAIL
ISBN 1-903568-10-2

THE LYKE WAKE WALK GUIDE
ISBN 1-903568-14-5

THE 1066 COUNTRY WALK
ISBN 1-903568-00-5

JOHN O'GROATS TO LANDS END

ISBN 1-903568-18-8

MILLENNIUM CYCLE RIDES IN 1066 COUNTRY (EAST SUSSEX)
ISBN 1-903568-04-8

TOURIST GUIDE TO VARADERO, CUBA
ISBN 1-903568-08-0

LANDS END TO JOHN O'GROATS CYCLE GUIDE

ISBN 1-903568-11-0

SHORT WALKS IN THE LAKE DISTRICT
ISBN 1-903568-20-X
FIRST PUBLISHED 2004
CHALLENGE PUBLICATIONS
7, EARLSMERE DRIVE, BARNSLEY. S71 5HH

Brian Smailes

Holds the record for the fastest 4 and 5 continuous crossings of the Lyke Wake Walk over the North York Moors. He completed the 210miles over rough terrain on 5 crossings in June 1995 taking 85hours and 50minutes.

His most recent venture was to walk from John O'Groats to Lands End, completing it in August 2003 in 34 days. In August 2001 he cycled from Lands End to John O'Groats, a journey of over 900miles in 6days 13hours 18minutes. This involved carrying food, clothing and tent, and was completed without support between both ends.

Brian lectures on outdoor pursuit courses and between these travels extensively on walking expeditions and projects around Great Britain.

Long distance running and canoeing are other sports he enjoys, completing 25 marathons and canoeing the Caledonian Canal 3 times.

Having travelled extensively throughout the UK, Europe and the Caribbean, Brian has recently been writing international travel guides to enable the holidaymaker to access the world with ease and enjoy it as much as he does.

Short Walks in the Lake District
ISBN 1-903568-20-X
First Published 2004
Published by: - Challenge Publications, 7 Earlsmere Drive, Barnsley, S71 5HH
Printed by: - Dearne Valley Printers Ltd. Tel: 01709 872188

The information recorded in this book is believed by the author to be correct at publication. No liabilities can be accepted for any inaccuracies, which may be found. It is recommended that anyone using this book should refer to the relevant map in conjunction with the walks described in this book and be experienced in map recognition and compass use.

The description or representation of a route used does not necessarily mean there is existence of a right of way.

CONTENTS

Page

Photographs

Walks	Grade	Time Hrs	Km
1 Lady's Rake & Derwent Water View	A-B	2½	5
2 Great Gable/Green Gable Circular	C	5	8.1
3. Scales Tarn	B	5½	8.4
4. Castlerigg Ancient Stone Circle	A	2½	9
5. Skiddaw Circular	B-C	7	13.6
6. Derwent Water Circular Walk	A	5	13.7
7. Scoat Tarn Circular	C	4¾	14.8
8. Low Rigg Circular	A	5¼	16.2
9. Wast Water View & Illgill Head	B	5½	17.2
10. Cat Bells/Dale Head via Ferry	C	6	17.4
11. Watendlath via Ashness Bridge	A-B	6	19.6
12. Helvellyn, Catstye Cam & Nethermost Pike	C	11	23

INTRODUCTION

This selection of both low and high level, short and longer distance walks have been chosen especially for those on holiday in the Lake District to enjoy within the bounds of their capability.

Those who are able to climb the heights will enjoy breathtaking views from the summits and ridges but even for people who enjoy low-level walks; the Lake District is picturesque, colourful and wherever you walk you will enjoy the scenery the peacefulness and the welcome that is The Lake district.

Difficulty   A = Easy   B = Moderate   C = Hard
Walk **1** =**A-B**   Walk **2 = C**   Walk **3 = B**   Walk **4 = A**
Walk **5 = B-C**   Walk **6 = A**   Walk **7 = C**   Walk **8 = A**
Walk **9 = B**   Walk **10 = C**   Walk **11 = A-B** Walk **12 = C**

Conversion
1Km   = 0.6214 mile
3Km   = 1.86 miles
8Km   = 4.97 miles
20Km = 12.43 miles

The maps required for these walks are: -
OS. Explorer No. OL4 for walks **1, 2, 4, 5, 6, 10, 11, Part of 7 & 8**
OS. Explorer No. OL5 for walks **3, 12, Part of 8**
OS. Explorer No. OL6 for walks **9, Part of 7**

Any compass bearings shown are given as magnetic.
Distances on all walks have been calculated to include ascents and descents.
A description of a route or track is not evidence of a right of way.

Walking times and distances given are approximate. Fitness, weight of rucksack, weather conditions and amount of climbing involved all affect your walking time. Please add extra time for stops on route.

EQUIPMENT SELECTION

Clothing should protect you from the elements as well as the changes in temperature that occur between the valley and the mountain track.

Boots
A good fitting pair of boots can make the difference between success and failure on any walk. Ankle protection is important especially where stones are found on the track throughout large parts of a route and where uneven ground can inflict injury very easily.

Most types of leather boots will need 'breaking-in' before use. Regular waxing will help keep the leather soft and supple. A sewn-in tongue will help prevent water and small stones getting into the boot. Before buying boots always try them on wearing the socks you will use with them. The boots should not be too tight as to cramp your toes, likewise not too slack that your feet move around inside.

Socks
Some walkers prefer to wear 2 pairs of socks, others only one. Whatever your choice they should ideally be approximately 60% wool for good insulating property. Some socks have a thick base to help cushion the feet. You can usually buy short, medium and long depending on preference.

Trousers
Should be loose fitting and ideally made of cotton or a fleece type of material. Cotton trousers will be light to wear, keep you warm and most importantly will dry quickly when wet. Fleece trousers will generally keep you very warm. They are lightweight and can be waterproofed.

Jeans are not suitable for walking at all as they take a long time to dry when wet and become very heavy. They can also chafe the skin, draw the body heat and their insulating property is very low.

Hat

Much of the body's heat is lost through the head, so some protection is strongly advised.

Jacket

Your jacket is one of the most important items as it will insulate your main body and help keep a constant body temperature. Fleece jackets are popular, as are breathable fabric jackets. A hood attached with a drawstring will give good protection around the head and full length two-way zips help to regulate body heat as well as allowing for ease in putting on/taking off in a harsh environment.

Many people buy breathable jackets, which are waterproof and windproof. When the outside becomes wet it ceases to be breathable and you may get condensation building up inside. These jackets are only breathable when dry, so choose carefully as they are expensive. Whichever jacket you buy, ensure it is waterproof and not just shower proof.

Features to look for on waterproof jackets are: -
- Full length two-way zip to help to regulate body heat and with putting on/taking off. It should also have a flap over it.
- Side pockets also with a flap over to stop water entering.
- Draw string on the fitted hood.
- Elasticated or adjustable cuffs to stop wind flow through the jacket at times of high wind or when cold.

Over Trousers

Waterproof/breathable trousers should have an elasticated waist and/or drawstring. Zips on the lower legs are very beneficial as these enable you to put them on/take off without taking your boots off. Do not wear them any longer than necessary as condensation can build up inside.

Gaiters

Help to protect the lower leg from wet or abrasive rock. When walking the routes described, I feel there is not a great need to wear them. Gaiters should be waterproof and ideally breathable.

Gloves

A pair of fleece or woollen gloves/mittens is strongly recommended in times of adverse weather. You will find that 5-finger gloves, as opposed to mittens, are probably better, especially in strong wind when handling map or adjusting compass.

Rucksack

This should be large enough to hold all your personal and safety equipment described. A rucksack should ideally have wide padded shoulder straps and a waist belt to stop it moving around. It is advisable to put a liner inside to keep your clothes and other items dry in very wet conditions. External zipped pockets in which to put small or frequently needed items i.e. water bottle, map, food etc are very useful.

Emergency Equipment

The following items may never be used but should always be carried in your rucksack. This includes spare clothing e.g. sweater, socks etc.

Torch
Pencil & Notebook
Whistle
Survival Bag
First Aid Kit (see First Aid Section).
Map/Compass

CHECKLIST   **Tick**

- Boots
- Socks
- Torch/Spare Bulb & Batteries
- Rucksack
- Whistle
- Hat
- Gloves
- Spare Clothing/Socks etc.
- First Aid Kit
- Maps/Compass
- Insect Repellent
- Sunscreen
- Toiletries
- Pencil/Notebook
- Waterproof/Windproofs
- Gaiters
- Water Bottle
- Survival Bag

FIRST AID

Knowledge of basic first aid would be helpful on any walk. In any accident or emergency situation, reassuring the casualty and comforting them is very important, do not move the casualty if the accident is of a possible serious nature e.g. a back or head injury. Ensure the casualty is warm then send for help. Someone should stay with the injured person. If the injury is not of a serious nature the injured person should, if and when possible, be removed from danger.

Where there is the possibility of shock or delayed shock, reassurance and company is vital. It is a fact that the majority of accidents happen on the return or second half of the journey. This is probably due to fatigue, cold or complacency.

Common Types of Injuries

Cuts and grazes	*Broken Arms/Legs*	*Cracked Ribs*
Blisters	*Hypothermia*	*Head Injuries*
Sprained Ankle/Wrist	*Sun Stroke*	*Gashed Shins*

All the above, however minor, can prove fatal with the casualty going into shock, especially in an exposed area or in times of panic, fog or adverse conditions, coupled with the injury.

In the event of an accident, 2 people should go for help; this should be the fittest person and best navigator. They should take their own personal safety equipment with them. Other people should stay with the injured person to help and reassure them.

Individual First Aid Kit

Adhesive Dressing	*Waterproof Container*
Triangular Bandage	*Sterile Dressing*
Bandage	*Crepe Bandage*
Safety Pins	*Gauze/Lint*
Scissors	*Micropore*
Insect Repellent	*Sun Cream*
Blister Treatments	

HYPOTHERMIA

Hypothermia is caused when the body core temperature falls below 35°C. If a walker is not properly prepared for the conditions or the equipment/clothing is not satisfactory then a combination of the cold, wet, exhaustion and the wind chill factor can give a walker hypothermia.

The Signs and Symptoms in Descending Order: -

Shivering
Cold, pale and dry skin
Low body temperature
Irrational behaviour
A gradual slip into unconsciousness
Pulse and respiratory rate slow
Difficulty in detecting breathing and pulse when unconscious
Death

Ways of Preventing Hypothermia

1. Build up body clothing in thin layers, adding on or taking off as necessary.
2. Have suitable wind/waterproofs with you.
3. Take some food/hot drink or boiled sweets, which produce energy and heat during digestion.
4. Wear a balaclava/woolly hat to insulate the head, and some gloves.
5. Shelter out of the wind.
6. Take a survival bag and if conditions dictate, use it. The temperature difference between the valley and the high ground can be several degrees. If the injured walker is able to move safely, descending to lower ground is usually the best solution.

When conditions do not permit movement and if you are in a sheltered area, stay where you are until such time as conditions improve. It may be at this time that you put on extra clothing and use survival bags.

Treatment for Hypothermia

1. Provide extra clothing and shelter from the elements.
2. Bodily warmth of others helps in a gradual warming.
3. If well enough come down into a warmer sheltered area.
4. Give hot drinks if conscious.
5. Give chocolate or sweets if the patient can still take food.
6. The casualty should be placed so that the head is slightly lower than the body.

DO NOT *rub the skin or use a hot water bottle as this can cause a surge of blood from the central body core to the surface, this could prove fatal.*

Alcohol should not be consumed on any walk and should not be given to anyone who has hypothermia. The body temperature will be lowered as well as giving a false sense of security.

THE COUNTRY CODE

The countryside is a place where many people like to escape to and enjoy at various times. To do this we need to look after it when we use it and to preserve it for future generations.

The following is a simple list of do's and don'ts to help everyone enjoy the countryside.

Do
- Guard against all risk of fire
- Fasten all gates
- Keep dogs under close control
- Use gates and stiles to cross walls and fences
- Protect wildlife, trees and plants
- Take litter home
- Leave nothing but footprints, take nothing but photographs
- Be conscious at all times of erosion of footpaths

Don't
- Play radios etc. or create unnecessary noise
- Take mountain bikes on walkways
- Touch machinery, livestock or crops

Walk from Keswick
Walk 1:   Lady's Rake & Derwent Water View
Allow 2½hrs   Difficulty = A-B   Distance 5km/3.1miles

This is a pleasant walk with excellent views of Derwent Water, Cat Bells to the south west, Helvellyn to the south east and Skiddaw to the north.

Leaving Keswick centre, walk through the town to the junction of the A591 (Brigham) and walk up Chestnut Hill, passing houses on both sides. Ascend to a minor road at the top of the hill on your right leading to Castlerigg. Turn right on the metalled road and walk to the far end, passing Castlerigg Hall Farm on your right and another farm on your left. To your right you can see Derwent Water.

You come to a house on your left, where a sign points right to Walla Crag. Soon after passing the house, cross over the footbridge on your right, taking you to the other side of the beck. Ascend the stony path to a stile. The beck is now below on your left and behind you there are excellent views of Keswick.

Cross the stile and ascend on the obvious grass and scree path. This path takes you to a stone wall on your right with a kissing gate, go through and continue to the summit. Lady's Rake GR. 275211 is 540yds further on. The path is narrow and winding, take care near the rake.

Look for a stile over the stone wall. Cross here, turning left and descending by the wall to the path you came on. Return to the minor road on this path then continue to the main road, turning left to return to Keswick.

Lady's Rake is named after the young wife of the Earl of Derwent Water. He was beheaded following the Jacobite rising of 1715.   His wife escaped by fleeing Lord's Island and climbing Walla Crag using this gully.

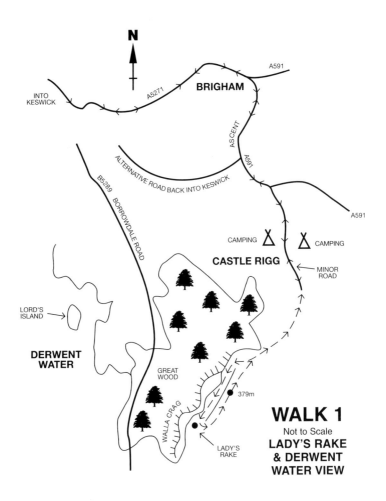

N

Walk from Seathwaite
Walk 2:   Great Gable/Green Gable Circular
Allow 5hrs   Difficulty = C   Distance 8.1km/5miles

A steady ascent up the valley from Seathwaite with excellent scenery heading towards Sty Head Tarn and a good picnic spot!

Starting from Seathwaite, park near the farm along the minor road from Seatoller Bridge at GR. 235123. Nearby is a small café and a trout farm. Go through a gate by the farm then continue to a stile and gate. Stay on the path into the distance *(Plate 1)* as you head up the valley. Cross a small bridge over Grains Gill and the path starts to ascend as you walk towards the head of the valley.

Follow the course of the gill on the undulating path and you come to a stile and gate. Cross the small but impressive stone packhorse bridge known as Stockley Bridge as you turn to the right. When you pass through the gate the path starts to ascend steeply. Go through a small gate in a stone wall then the obvious path bears off to the right.

Looking back at night towards Seathwaite you can often see a small light at the farm there. This is a guide for any walkers returning at night by this route, especially in bad weather.

Approaching the head of the valley, the path flattens a little. A waterfall (Taylorgill Force) runs on your right and the path becomes very uneven and wet in parts. The path turns slightly left between the head of the two hills. It is important to keep Styhead Gill on your right as you ascend.

The path along by the gill is very uneven with large stones and difficult to walk over. There is a cairn on the level area between the two hills. It may be surrounded by water in extreme conditions but is a good route marker. A bridge which you cross is approx 86yds ahead of the cairn.

You now walk on the right side of the gill and the path can be wet here. Continue ascending to another cairn off to you left then just past it cross a stream again still on the main path. You soon pass by Sty Head Tarn on your left. Cross over the gill again where it is better to walk. The path starts to divide nearing the head of the valley and it is important to head for the large rocks you see in front of you. You arrive at a mountain rescue first aid stretcher box.

Look now for a path on your right which ascends steeply to the summit of Great Gable for 1625yds. Arriving beside the cairn on the summit of Great Gable (there is no 'trig' point here), turn right on a general bearing of 58°M from the summit walking for 866yds around Gable Crag onto the summit of Green Gable.

On the summit of Green Gable, walk on bearing 66°M for 2.1miles back to Seathwaite, descending gradually on a path between crags in an anti-clockwise direction initially around the summit of Base Brown into the valley at Gillercomb then clockwise on the path emerging beside Seathwaite Farm where you started. Turn left back to the road where you parked.

WALK 2
Not to Scale
GREAT GABLE/GREEN GABLE CIRCULAR

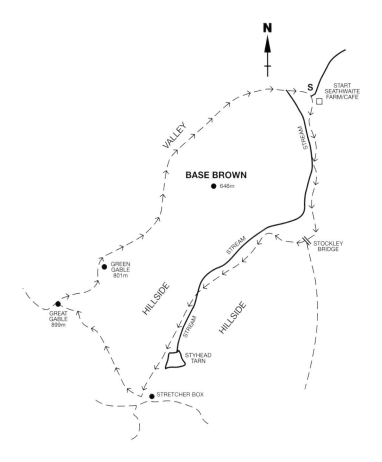

N

START
SEATHWAITE
FARM/CAFE

S

VALLEY

STREAM

BASE BROWN
● 646m

STREAM

STOCKLEY
BRIDGE

STREAM

GREEN
GABLE
801m

HILLSIDE

HILLSIDE

GREAT
GABLE
899m

STREAM

STYHEAD
TARN

● STRETCHER BOX

Walk from Scales near Threlkeld
Walk 3:   Scales Tarn
Allow 5½hrs   Difficulty = B   Distance 8.4km/5.2miles

A nice but strenuous walk up the hillside. Once on top, a gentler walk to Scales Tarn and a pleasant, sheltered picnic area. Good views all round.

Starting beside the public house at Scales, GR. 343269. Turn right bearing 70°M walking along the minor road for 760yds to a sheepfold on your left. Turn left to ascend a path keeping a wall on your left and ascends initially for 300yds then as the path veers left, continue ascending a narrow path which winds clockwise up the mountainside. You should see the ascending path ahead.

Continue right to the top then as the ground levels out on the ridge, turn left on bearing 264°M walking for 1.1miles on a narrow, feint path between the mountainsides, keeping the narrow river just off to your right. As you slightly veer away from the river and meet crags at the far end, pick up a narrow path ascending the hillside steeply on your left.

Continue up for 325yds then as the path levels you should see Scales Tarn nestling at the foot of Tarn Crags at GR. 329281. Walk to the tarn taking care not to swim in the ice-cold water. The tarn is surrounded with towering slopes so is sheltered to a large extent from the wind. Return by the same route back to Scales.

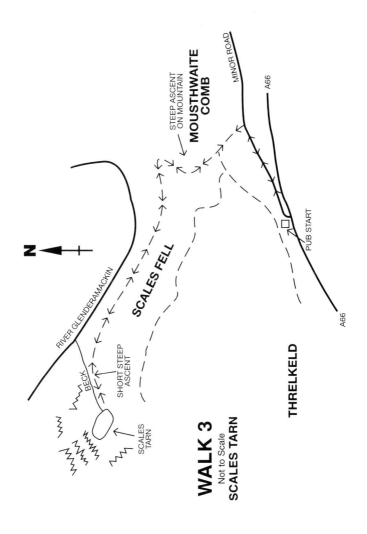

WALK 3
Not to Scale
SCALES TARN

N

MOUSTHWAITE COMB

STEEP ASCENT ON MOUNTAIN

SCALES FELL

MINOR ROAD

A66

A66

PUB START

THRELKELD

RIVER GLENDERAMACKIN

BECK

SHORT STEEP ASCENT

SCALES TARN

Walk from Keswick
Walk 4:   Castlerigg Ancient Stone Circle
Allow 2½hrs   Difficulty = A   Distance 9km/5.5miles

This stone circle is thought to be 4000 years old and around 100 feet in diameter, consisting of 38 megalithic stones with an oblong space of 10 further stones inside. Good views of Skiddaw and surrounding area from here.

Leaving Keswick centre, walk on the footpath through the town on the A5271 to the junction of the A591 (Brigham) and walk up Chestnut Hill, passing houses on both sides. Ascend to a minor road near the top of the hill on your right leading to Castlerigg. Turn right onto the metalled road and walk for 765yds passing the farm, to a kissing gate on your left. Go through and continue alongside a wall to some steps over a stone wall.

Turn left descending slightly down the side of several fields to the main A591 road. Cross with care onto Castle Lane, which is a minor road. Walk for 1080yds on this metalled road to a sign on your right going through the gate leading to Castlerigg Stone Circle GR. 291236 *(Plate 2)*.

Leave the stone circle by the other gate nearby. Turn left passing the car park and walk on the minor road for 1400yds back towards Keswick, to emerge near the junction of Chestnut Hill.

Turn left to the junction then left again ascending Chestnut Hill for 750yds, to the first main road on your right. This road leads back into the centre of Keswick, and is a pleasant walk on a quieter road.

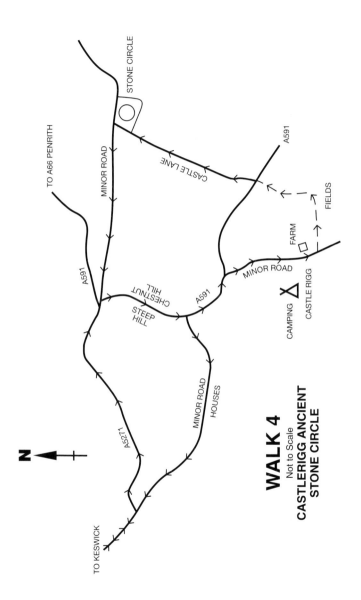

WALK 4
Not to Scale
CASTLERIGG ANCIENT
STONE CIRCLE

18

Walk from Applethwaite.
Walk 5:   Skiddaw Circular
Allow 7hrs   Difficulty = B-C   Distance 13.6km/8.4miles

A good exhilarating walk but with a tough ascent then descent back to Applethwaite. It is a safe walk but can be testing when windy on the ascent and on the summit.

Leaving Applethwaite take the public footpath that runs parallel with the road from Applethwaite to Millbeck Farm in a north westerly direction in total about 760yds. Turn right, through the farm buildings to Millbeck then Benny Crag and pick up the path that ascends steeply to the summit of Skiddaw.

You can follow the easier route of the Allerdale Ramble all the way from Millbeck to Skiddaw if you chose to. When you pass Carlside Tarn the final ascent to Skiddaw is very stony and steep. The presence of strong winds here makes the ascent more dangerous so take care particularly from the tarn to the summit. The 'trig' point number is S1543. There is a wind shelter on the summit.

Leaving the 'trig' point return on the same path for 650yds, then bear left at the fork in the path, bearing 130°M to leave Little Man summit off to your right. The path here is stony. Further ahead you come to a stile. Go over this then bear right descending *(Plate 3)* to a car park by a forest. The path should now be clearly visible as you descend.

Go through a kissing gate then turn right to the car park. At the car park turn right and walk for 1.2miles on the yellow 'B' road along the north side of the forest back to Applethwaite.

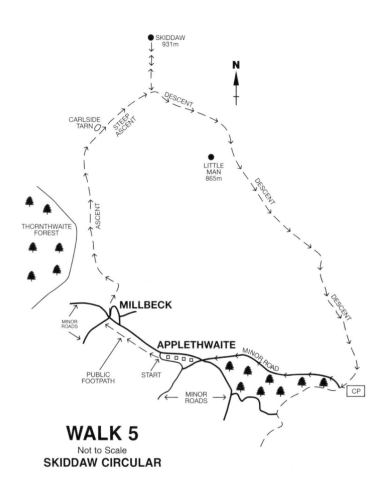

WALK 5
Not to Scale
SKIDDAW CIRCULAR

Walk from Keswick
Walk 6:   Derwent Water Circular
Allow 5hrs   Difficulty = A   Distance 13.7Km/8.4miles

Derwent Water is just over 3 miles long and 1 mile wide. This walk is relatively flat, enabling you to see the lake closely and enjoy the scenery around its shoreline. There are numerous picnic stops around the lakeside. A ferry is available back from Hawes End if you prefer.

Leaving from Keswick T.I.C., follow signs south towards the lakeside and landing stages, bearing right by George Fisher outdoor shop to the lake, passing the park on route.

At the landing stage GR. 264227, continue on a narrow metalled road/path around the lake. Keep to the obvious paths, some signed. On seeing a sign for Kettlewell car park after passing the youth hostel, cross the road, the sign there states that the path rejoins the road further on. Take this route, which leads through the wood emerging near Mary Mount Hotel. Continue, passing the Lodore Hotel on your left.

Walk on the footpath where possible until you see a public footpath sign for Manesty leading towards the lake GR. 264187. Follow this path across the field passing over a footbridge then on a boarded walkway over the wet area.

You meet the Allerdale Ramble path. Turn right on this well-defined path leading around the lakeside. At a house called 'The Warren' turn right through a 5-bar gate towards Abbot's Bay then through a kissing gate near a white house at Brandelhow. Much of this section is through woods near the lakeside.

Pass through another kissing gate near a landing stage taking the left path. Go through another kissing gate and over a stile then take the right hand path to Hawes End GR. 249213. You can either continue around the lake or take the ferry back to the landing stage near Keswick from here.

If continuing around the lake, walk up to the road, turn right then descend a short distance to a kissing gate on the right following a sign to Keswick. Cross the field on the distinctive path then through another kissing gate. You emerge at the side of a house. Cross the driveway following the footpath to Keswick.

The path forks soon after, take the left path through the wood to emerge at the road near Nichol End Marine. Turn right walking on the footpath towards Keswick. Just past the village store GR. 252235, turn right passing Derwent Hill centre then over a footbridge crossing the river. Walk on the metalled road to a public footpath sign to Keswick through a small gate.

Continue on the straight path to the far end as you enter Keswick, emerging opposite the Cumberland Pencil factory. Turn right to walk back into Keswick centre.

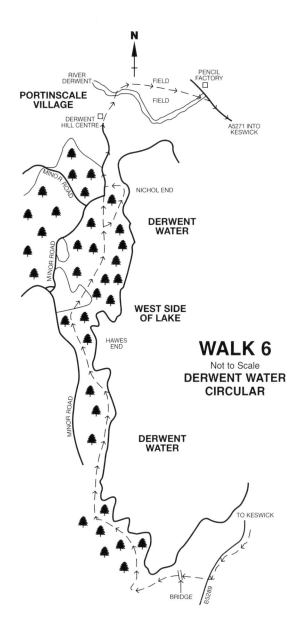

N

RIVER
DERWENT

FIELD

PENCIL
FACTORY

**PORTINSCALE
VILLAGE**

FIELD

DERWENT
HILL CENTRE

A5271 INTO
KESWICK

MINOR ROAD

NICHOL END

**DERWENT
WATER**

MINOR ROAD

**WEST SIDE
OF LAKE**

HAWES
END

WALK 6
Not to Scale
**DERWENT WATER
CIRCULAR**

MINOR ROAD

**DERWENT
WATER**

TO KESWICK

B5289

BRIDGE

23

Walk from Overbeck Bridge Car Park, Wast Water
Walk 7:   Scoat Tarn Circular
Allow 4¾hrs   Difficulty = C   Distance 14.8km/9.1miles

A good but demanding circular walk covering the peaks of Red Pike, Scoat Fell and Haycock with impressive views throughout.

Leaving the car park at Overbeck Bridge, take the footpath from the back of the car park and ascend an obvious path through two gates.

After the second gate turn right, ascending steeply, keeping to the left of the wall. The path divides after 542yds, take the left fork passing under Dropping Crag, and then follow this path all the way up the valley to Dore Head. There are good views into Mosedale and up to Pillar.

On reaching Dore Head, turn left following the steep path up to the summit of Red Pike. Just past Red Pike you can see Scoat Tarn in the valley to your left. From here the path drops a little then contours around N.W. to GR. 158113 (stone wall). There is a nice, short but worthwhile excursion out to the summit of Steeple at GR. 157116.

Head N.N.W. to Steeple on the path for 433yds then return to the path junction again. Bear 246°M on another short trip of 1625yds which will take you over Scoat Fell to the summit of Haycock giving you good views of the Irish Sea and I.o.M. on a clear day.

Return 480yds to the path junction at GR. 148109 then bear 148°M to descend by Nether Beck into the valley on a gradual descent to the road at Netherbeck Bridge. Turn left at the road walking 760yds back to the car park.

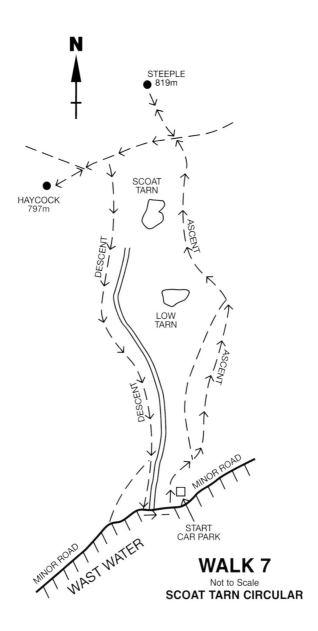

N

STEEPLE
● 819m

SCOAT
TARN

HAYCOCK
797m

DESCENT

ASCENT

LOW
TARN

DESCENT

ASCENT

MINOR ROAD

START
CAR PARK

MINOR ROAD

WAST WATER

WALK 7
Not to Scale
SCOAT TARN CIRCULAR

Walk from Keswick Centre
Walk 8:   Low Rigg Circular
Allow 5¼hrs   Difficulty = A   Distance 16.2km/10miles

A mostly flat walk along a disused railway line and over paths and fields with only a small amount of climbing. Good views of the River Greta as you walk along the railway line and through the wooded areas.

From Keswick centre walk along the A5271 in an easterly direction towards Brigham and Chestnut Hill. Keep the River Greta on your left. Cross the first road bridge where it passes over the old railway. Continue a further 650yds to the second bridge over the old railway 160yds before the junction with the A591.

Just before the bridge, turn left descending some steps at the side of the bridge onto a path. Bear left walking for 140yds near the Keswick by-pass then turn right by the small industrial estate there towards the old railway line running under the by-pass at GR. 282239. When you are near the by-pass descend a path with a handrail, onto the old railway line heading in an easterly direction towards Threlkeld.

Go through a gate onto the good flat track, which crosses several bridges over the river. Continue on this track for 2.1miles to the A66 road. Turn left at the road walking on the footpath for 270yds to a sign stating 'Threlkeld ¼mile'. Follow the sign into Threlkeld where food and drinks are available at the inns there.

Beside the Horse & Farrier Inn is St.Mary's Church in the centre of Threlkeld at GR. 322254. Look for the public footpath sign at the side of the church leading down a farm track for 270yds to a stile. Cross then walk diagonally across the field to the main road. Cross the busy road with care to the stile at the far side. Continue on the winding path, crossing a stile onto a track.

Plate 1

View showing the distinct path from Seathwaite ascending to Sty Head Tarn.
To the right is Stockley Bridge in Walk No. 2

Plate 2
Castlerigg Stone Circle in Walk No. 4

28

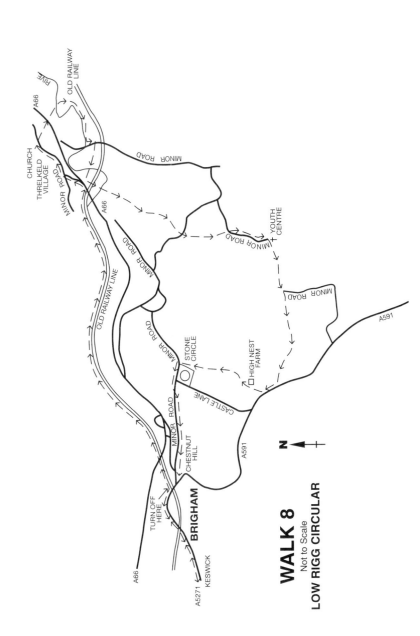

WALK 8
Not to Scale
LOW RIGG CIRCULAR

29

Look for a wooden platform over a beck, which you cross then cross a stile at the side of a field, staying on the visible path. Cross another stile to Mill Bridge then cross the bridge and turn immediately right through a kissing gate into a field. Walk around the edge of the field into the next field. Go through a gate into the next field then turn right walking on a track towards a farm keeping a row of houses off to your left.

Continue ahead, passing the farm at GR. 322247 to a road at the far side of the caravan site. At the road, go straight across following a small sign stating 'Railway Footpath Keswick'. Go through a gate, then a kissing gate and continue along the railway line over Threlkeld Bridge to the minor road. Turn left along the road, crossing a bridge.

Just past a bungalow on your left, turn left at a public footpath sign; go through a kissing gate, cross the middle of the field to an opening in the fence at the far side. Cross several fields through kissing gates and two 5-bar gates leading to Shundraw Farm at GR. 308236.

At the right side of the farm a sign states 'St. John's Church'. Follow this through two 5-bar gates alongside a stone wall to an opening in the wall. Follow the yellow arrow and path to a white farm at Row End, and then continue to Yew Tree Farm. Walk along the metalled road ascending to St. John's Church and youth centre at GR. 307225.

Just opposite the church is an opening in the wall leading to Low Rigg, a short distance away. After visiting Low Rigg return to St. John's Church and continue on the road over the hillside leading onto a track towards Dale Bottom.

The track winds around the hillside then meets a minor road. Go straight across through a kissing gate onto a public footpath. Descend over rock to another kissing gate, then over a large field following a sign towards Keswick. Cross a small wooden bridge then at another sign turn right on an obvious track *(Plate 4)* ascending through two fields to the main A591 road at Nest Brow.

Plate 3
Looking back to Skiddaw showing the distinct path descending to near
'Whit Beck', Near the Car Park in Walk No. 5.

31

Plate 4

Skiddaw in the background

Your route in the foreground takes you near Dale Bottom Camp Site on route to Nest Brow in Walk No. 8.

Turn right on the A591, walking 50yds up the road, turn right over a cattle grid then immediately left through a farm gate, a large tree is on your left side. Cross another cattle grid and walk along the metalled access road. Pass High Nest Farm on your right then go through a gate. Keep a stone wall on your right then cross three sets of ladder steps over stone walls as you cross four fields.

You emerge on a minor road by some trees with Castlerigg Stone Circle just off to your left. Turn left on the minor road, stopping for a visit to the stone circle then walking 1.4Km past High Fieldside Farm to the main A591 road. Turn left and continue on the A5271main road back into Keswick.

Walk from 'The Green', Wasdale Head
Walk 9:   Wast Water View & Illgill Head Circular
Allow 5½hrs   Difficulty = B   Distance 17.2km/10.6miles

A low and high-level walk. Care must be taken along by the screes at the bottom in wet weather and at the top in windy weather. Good views of all the surrounding hills and sea beyond on this exhilarating walk.

Leaving 'The Green' at Wasdale Head, bear left by the old school house. The path takes you over the river and along the left side of the National Trust campsite towards Wast Water.

You come to a wooden bridge over the beck. Cross the bridge where a signpost points right to the lakeshore. Follow the wide farm track then a narrow path around the left side of the lake. The scree is banking up steeply now to your left with Wast Water to your right.

Approximately ⅔ of the way along, the path can be very slippery as you scramble over the rocks. Take extra care here particularly if it is wet, allowing extra time for your walk.

You come to a building at the end of the lake known as the pump-house. continue on the track past the pump-house for 216yds to a 5-bar gate with a kissing gate beside it. Do not go through but bear left alongside a stone wall. A small sign states 'To Fell'.

The path ascends slightly by the stone wall before turning left and climbing steeply up the side of Greathall Gill by a line of trees. Follow the distinct path approx. 1000yds to the top.

When you meet another path at the top, turn left on bearing 68°M on a path heading northeast above the screes and over Whin Rigg. Continue for 1.8miles to the 'trig' point on Illgill Head where there is also a cairn. It is important not to venture left to the screes.

Plate 5

View looking back to the A591 and the ascent with Bridge End Camp Site hidden behind the trees (Top right).
Your path is in the foreground ascending to Raise - in Walk No. 12.

Plate 6
View looking back from Lower Man to Whiteside Bank
on route to Helvellyn on Walk No. 2

Continue on the main path bearing 68°M from the 'trig' point for approx. 1.2miles until you meet another distinct path from Burnmoor Tarn leading to Fence Wood. Turn left at this path to descend to the northern end of Wast Water via a path which skirts the east side of Fence Wood.

You rejoin the path beside the bridge at Brackenclose then retrace your steps along by the campsite to 'The Green' at Wasdale Head.

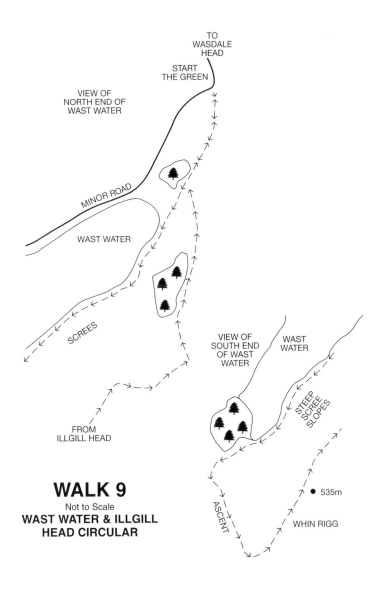

TO
WASDALE
HEAD

START
THE GREEN

VIEW OF
NORTH END OF
WAST WATER

MINOR ROAD

WAST WATER

SCREES

VIEW OF
SOUTH END
OF WAST
WATER

WAST
WATER

STEEP
SCREE
SLOPES

FROM
ILLGILL HEAD

ASCENT

● 535m

WHIN RIGG

WALK 9
Not to Scale
WAST WATER & ILLGILL
HEAD CIRCULAR

Plate 7
Helvellyn Summit with Ullswater in Background in Walk No. 12

Plate 8
View from Helvellyn to Nethermost Pike showing the distinct path up to the summit.
The path off to the right leads down to the A591 and Thirlmere.

Walk from Keswick
Walk 10:   Cat Bells/Dalehead Horseshoe
Allow 6hrs   Difficulty = C   Distance 17.4km/10.8 miles

This walk has some steep ascents and descents, is very strenuous but gives some of the best views in the Lake District from Cat Bells looking over Derwent Water and again from Maiden Moor looking into the dale and across to High Seat.

Start as Derwent Water circular walk No.6 walking to the landing stages near Keswick.

At the landing stage take the ferry to Hawes End, (ferry times available from the TIC in the town centre) on the opposite side of the lake; alternatively walk to Hawes End via Portinscale. From the ferry landing at Hawes End, walk straight ahead through a kissing gate and follow the path to the road. Turn right to a small car park where a sign points left through the trees to Cat Bells. Ascend by the wall to another car park then onto the road crossing a cattle grid GR. 247212. Continue a short distance to a signpost on a sharp hairpin bend at the foot of Cat Bells. Look ahead for a path ascending Cat Bells. This ascends steeply to the summit on a well-defined scree path.

Continue over the summit where you will see a path descending then ascending steeply up the mountainside. Do not take the other paths leading off left and right. Ascend to Bull Crag on the scree path. Stay on the obvious path crossing over Maiden Moor which leads to High Spy summit. You have excellent views of Dale Head and Hindscarth off to your right and of Newlands Beck below in the dale.

Approaching High Spy you can see the distinctive cairn on the summit. Leaving High Spy take extra care on the rock strewn path, GR. 233157, leading to Dalehead Tarn below. Descend to the stream, cross then walk to the tarn where you bear right, to ascend very steeply GR. 228152 to Dale Head summit. A cairn marks the summit and you can see Buttermere in the distance behind.

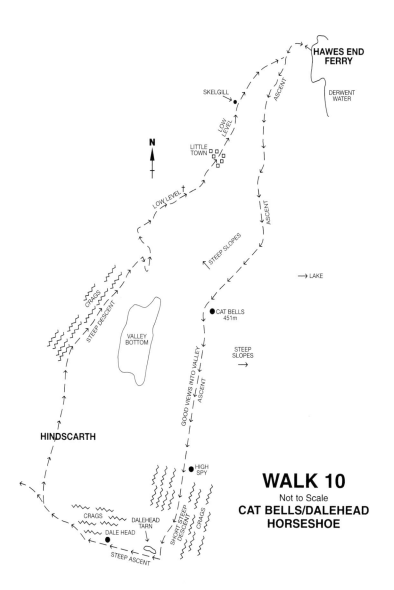

HAWES END
FERRY

DERWENT
WATER

SKELGILL

ASCENT

LOW
LEVEL

N

LITTLE
TOWN

LOW LEVEL

ASCENT

STEEP SLOPES

→ LAKE

CRAGS

STEEP DESCENT

VALLEY
BOTTOM

CAT BELLS
451m

STEEP
SLOPES
→

GOOD VIEWS INTO VALLEY

ASCENT

HINDSCARTH

HIGH
SPY

WALK 10
Not to Scale
**CAT BELLS/DALEHEAD
HORSESHOE**

CRAGS

DALEHEAD
TARN

SHORT STEEP DESCENT

CRAGS

DALE HEAD

STEEP ASCENT

Walk on the main path in the same direction along the summit ridge towards Hindscarth. Where the path divides take the right path onto Hindscarth summit GR. 215162. There are two wind shelters on the summit. The descent is steep and stony so extreme care needs to be taken. It is an obvious narrow path, which should be attempted slowly and carefully.

At the base of Hindscarth there is a 5-bar gate next to a farm building. A sign states 'Path to Newlands Church'. Follow this track for 466yds over the fields to the church that has an old school attached to it. Turn right on the narrow road, then at a junction cross the packhorse bridge into Little Town.

Just as you reach the houses a sign next to a 5-bar gate on the right states 'National Trust'. Go through the gate onto the track then bear left leading towards Cat Bells again. Stay on this main, low level track; do not ascend into the hills again. Walk for 1.4miles along the base of Cat Bells GR. 240196 to Skelgill, then onto a metalled road leading back to the cattle grid near Hawes End. Retrace your steps back to Hawes End landing.

When you reach the landing stages near Keswick where you started from, retrace your steps into the town centre.

Walk from Keswick
Walk 11:   Watendlath via Ashness Bridge
Allow 6hrs   Difficulty = A - B   Distance 19.6km/12.2 miles

This walk offers excellent viewing from the fells, leading to a delightful walk along by the beck in the dale, with numerous waterfalls. There is some climbing mainly at the beginning and end but worth the effort.

Leaving Keswick centre, walk through the town to the junction of the A591 (Brigham) and walk up Chestnut Hill, passing the houses on both sides. Ascend to a minor road on your right near the top of the hill, leading to Castlerigg. Turn right onto the metalled road and walk to the far end of it, passing Castlerigg Hall Farm on your right and another farm on your left.

You come to a house on your left, where a sign points right to Walla Crag. Soon after passing the house, cross over the footbridge on your right, taking you to the other side of the beck. Ascend the stony path to a stile. The beck is below now on your left and behind there are excellent views of Keswick.

Cross the stile and ascend on the obvious grass and scree path. This path takes you to a stone wall on your right with a kissing gate, go through and continue to the summit, just before Lady's Rake. Just over the summit as you start to descend, the path divides. A pile of stones marks the spot GR. 275207. Turn left here, do not go straight ahead. Bleaberry Fell is off to your left with Derwent Water to your right. Continue on this path, which again divides and you take the right hand path. Walk on the grass and peat path over a large open area of fell which turns to a stony track as you descend to Ashness Bridge.

The mountain at the other side of the lake on your right is Cat Bells GR. 244198. The path forks again, one descending and the other taking the higher ground bearing left, take this path. You can see Ashness Bridge below as you gradually descend on the distinctive path to it at GR. 270197.

Next to the bridge is The Bark House Mountain Base. Bear left on the metalled road at Ashness Bridge continuing on this narrow undulating road for 3miles to Watendlath, passing Ashness Cottage and crossing the two cattle grids at both ends of Ashness Wood. You arrive in the small village of Watendlath with the picturesque waterfalls and the packhorse bridge in the centre GR. 276163.

Cross the packhorse bridge, turning right through a wooden gate onto a path taking you back along the course of the river. There are numerous small waterfalls and fells on both sides. The scree path winds around a nab and ascends slightly on an obvious path before descending back near the beck. Go through two small gates then onto a flat grass path near the beck. You return onto the scree track then go through a kissing gate onto a good path near the river before crossing a footbridge spanning a wet area. Continue by the river to a wooden footbridge across the main beck, which you cross. Turn left through a gate on a forest track ascending through Ashness Wood. This leads back to the metalled road running through the wood. Turn left back to Ashness Bridge.

Cross the bridge, and then take the path off to your right just past the bridge. Do not return on the path you came on. Ascend this path to a wooden gate; go through then where the path divides take the narrow left path, which is scree and undulating through the ferns. Do not turn off this main path.

You enter Great Wood walk until you come to a wall, bear right ascending steeply through the wood. Cross a narrow wooden footbridge then go straight on for 800yds, do not ascend on the path to your right, which leads very steeply up to Lady's Rake. Go through a gate and continue on the obvious path bearing right soon after on a well defined track for 745yds to another path running left to right. A mast is just off to your left but turn right here at the path junction walking for 270yds to the road. Turn left at the road back towards the main A591 road.

Continue along the lane then turn left on meeting the A591, descending the road towards Keswick. Walk for 596yds to a road off to your left where you turn and continue into Keswick centre passing St. John's Church on route.

TO KESWICK

A5271

A591

CHESTNUT HILL

A591

NORTH END OF ROUTE

CASTLERIGG

RAKEFOOT FARM

FORD

TO KESWICK

BORROWDALE ROAD

GREAT WOOD

WALLA CRAG

WALK 11

Not to Scale

WATENDLATH VIA ASHNESS BRIDGE

DERWENT WATER

CAT GHYLL

ROAD TO ASHNESS BRIDGE

SOUTH END OF ROUTE

ASHNESS WOOD

TO BLEABERRY FELL

YOUTH HOSTEL

ROAD

WATENDLATH BECK

MINOR ROAD

ASHNESS BRIDGE

ROAD

TO WATENDLATH

WATENDLATH BECK

MINOR ROAD

PATH

WATENDLATH

SOUTH END

TARN

Walk from Thirlmere

Walk 12: Helvellyn (Catstye Cam & Nethermost Pike optional)

Allow 11hrs (full route)   5hrs for Helvellyn only

Difficulty = C   Distance23km/14.9miles

This walk has some steep ascents and descents but you are rewarded with superb views from the summits. When walking the full route you cross over some pinnacles along Swirral Edge and Striding Edge.

Starting from Highpark Wood car park just off A591 by Thirlmere, walk to the road. Turn right on the A591 towards Bridge End in a northerly direction. Walk for 1.2miles to a right turning towards St. John's in the Vale. Take the narrow metalled road signposted Glenridding via Sticks Pass.

The metalled road starts to ascend past Stybeck Caravan Site with a farm building on your left. Ahead is a sign to Sticks Pass near some ladder steps over a wall. Ascend a steep grass path *(Plate 5)* to a farm gate with a large outcrop of rock behind it. Cross a stile and through three gates following the ascending path over a small water channel before crossing a bridge over the stream.

A sign points to public footpath & Swales car park, but take the path on your left (which is almost due east), not the one to the car park. You ascend steeply now on a loose stone and grass path, passing a waterfall on your left. Once up the steep section, the walking becomes easier as you reach a grass plateau.

On meeting another path crossing left to right, turn right walking a further 1080yds to Raise summit, which has a small stone outcrop on top. The path immediately before the summit is steep with large stones scattered on it. In the distance behind you is Bassenthwaite Lake and Skiddaw. Once on the summit of Raise the path is clear ahead of you bearing 221°M.

After descending from Raise you drop down to Whiteside Bank then up to Low Man *(Plate 6),* which is the start of the ridge up to Helvellyn. The path is very stony but obvious.

Optional extra route

On the summit of Helvellyn beside the 'trig' point *(Plate 7)* retrace your steps a short distance to the start of Swirral Edge, which is marked by a pile of stones. Extreme care should be taken as you descend, bearing 57°M towards Catstye Cam. This route has a lot of loose stones and you can slip in wet conditions. When descending Swirral Edge, it is slightly easier to descend the right path, as the left is exposed and more difficult. As you scramble up to the summit of Catstye Cam Red Tarn is in the valley to your right. Retrace your steps, taking a left fork to descend the hillside towards Red Tarn.

Cross the stream at the bottom then bear 112°M towards a stone wall. At this point turn sharp right to go along Striding Edge. The path is very undulating and stony with steep drops off on both sides, but with care, most people can manage this section. Work your way along as you head back to Helvellyn summit.

Across to your right you have a good view of Swirral Edge and Catstye Cam. In front the sharp ascent to the summit can be seen. On the summit of Helvellyn after leaving Striding Edge there is a memorial dating from 1890 dedicated to a walker who died there. At this point bear 195°M towards Nethermost Pike *(Plate 8).* At a fork in the path, keep left to the summit now bearing 165°M. There are a number of piles of stones to guide you the short distance to the summit.

When leaving Nethermost Pike, retrace your steps to the previous fork in the path *(Plate 8)* then turn left by a pile of stones to descend Birk Side to the forest below. Descending you go around a rocky outcrop before the path reaches the forest. Just past this rocky outcrop, keep on the main right hand path rather than the small path to your left.

The descending path has a lot of loose stone. As it descends to the forest you come to a gate. A sign points to 'Thirlmere Swirls' on the right, take this path through the forest, it is narrow and undulating in parts but an excellent forest walk where you may see rabbits and deer. Continue on this path for 2.4miles back to the car park at High Park Wood at the northern end of the forest.

WALK 12
Not to Scale
HELVELLYN,
CATSTYE CAM &
NETHERMOST PIKE
(OPTIONAL)

TO KESWICK
A591

STEEP ASCENT

STICKS PASS

PUBLIC
HOUSE

A591

BUSY ROAD

RAISE
883m

WHITE
SIDE

C.P.
START

HELVELLYN
SCREES

ASCENT

CATSTYE
CAM
890m

TAKE CARE
HERE

SWIRRAL
EDGE

OPTIONAL
ROUTE

HELVELLYN
949m

RED
TARN

THIRLMERE
RESERVOIR

DESCENT

STRIDING EDGE
TAKE EXTRA CARE HERE

NETHERMOST
PIKE 891m

DESCENT

A591
TO GRASMERE

Bad Visibility Descents

Great Gable

Walk from the summit on a bearing of 235°M, descending on a winding path for 1700yds before turning onto a bearing of 258°M, follow this path for 1.2miles back to Wasdale Head.

Skiddaw

Walk from the triangulation pillar on a bearing of 185°M for 600yds, then bear left on a longer but definitely safer path descending on bearing 130°M. Taking the alternative path known as the Allerdale Ramble, takes you on a very stony windswept and dangerous path.

High Spy

From the summit of High Spy GR. 234162 walk on a bearing of 199°M for 620yds on a very stony steep descent to just before Dalehead Tarn.

Turn left at the junction on an obvious path bearing 130°M for 280yds, then on bearing 83°M for a further 488yds. Walk on bearing 104°M again for 280yds to join a definite farm track leading towards Rosthwaite where there is a telephone near a road leading back to Derwent Water.

Helvellyn

Walk from the triangulation pillar on a bearing of 304°M for 1.1miles, then on a bearing of 340°M for 760yds. These bearings will bring you back on a public footpath to the corner of Highpark Wood at GR. 320167, where you follow the descending path to the A591 road.

Catstye Cam

Walk from the summit on a bearing of 226°M for 540yds then pick up the path on your left on a bearing of 87°M to take you downhill to Red Tarn. When on the path at the tarn, take a bearing of 57°M to take you on the path back to Glenridding.

Nethermost Pike

Walk from the summit on a bearing of 352°M for 270yds then turn left bearing 209°M following a distinct zigzag path downhill. The path skirts then passes through a forest before meeting the A591 road beside Thirlmere.

These bad visibility descents, if used will take you to lower ground and safety, but not necessarily to your intended route destination.

Heights of Peaks

Great Gable	2922 ft
Green Gable	2603 ft
Skiddaw	3054 ft
High Spy	2047 ft
Dale Head	2437 ft
Red Pike	2684 ft
Steeple	2662 ft
Haycock	2590 ft
Illgill Head	1963 ft
Cat Bells	1465 ft
Helvellyn	3117 ft
Catstye Cam	2920 ft
Nethermost Pike	2923 ft

Mountain Rescue Posts

Wasdale Head   GR. 187088
Stretcher Box near Sty Head Tarn GR. 219095

GLOSSARY OF WORDS

Beck - *Cumbrian word for stream or brook or watercourse.*

Cairn - *An ancient stone mound erected as a marker. Often modern day piles of stones that denote a path or route are referred to as cairns.*

Dale - *Valley*

Escape Route - *Used for any emergency situation or in times of bad visibility.*

Fell - *Mountain/Hill*

Force - *Waterfall*

Gill - *Stream or beck*

Gyll - *Gully*

Grid Reference - *Derived from the national grid reference system, Used to pinpoint a place on a map by use of letters and numbers.*

Gully - *A narrow channel or cleft in a rock face, may have waterfalls and can be very slippery and have vertical drops.*

Kissing Gate - *Swing gate that usually lets one person through it at a time by moving the gate backwards and forwards.*

Metalled Road - *Generally known as a stone chipping road. This term evolved and became regarded as the roads metal or the roads surface.*

Nab - *Projecting spur*

Outcrop - *Part of a rock formation that sticks out from the main body of rock.*

Rake - *Gully*

Route Card - *A plan of action prepared before you leave. A copy to be left with someone so that if you fail to return by a planned time then help can be summoned.*

Scree - *Loose stone*

Summit - *The highest point of a mountain or hill.*

Thwaite - *Clearing in wood.*

Tarn - *A small mountain lake.*

Trig Point - *Triangulation Pillar. These mark the summit of many mountains but not all. It is a small stone pillar with a number on it. The height of the mountain is taken from this point.*

USEFUL ADDRESSES/TEL. No's

Long Distance Walkers Association
Les Maple
21 Upcroft,
Windsor,
Berks. SL4 3NH
Tel. 01753 866685

This association is set up to further the interests of those who enjoy long distance walking. Members receive a journal three times each year, which includes information on all aspects of long distance walking.

Ramblers Association
2nd Floor, Camelford House,
87-90 Albert Embankment,
London
 SE1 7TW
Tel. 01577 861222

Advice and information on all walking matters. Local groups, regular meetings.

National Parks Information Centre (Keswick)
Tel. 017687 72645

Hopefully you have enjoyed this selection of walks and gained as much pleasure from walking the routes as I did. Should you wish to walk other routes, please visit Challenge Publications website at: -

www.chall-pub.fsnet.co.uk

A wide selection of walking guides covering the UK are available including 'The National Three Peaks Walk'. The top selling and main book covering the famous three peaks routes and containing everything you need to know to complete the challenge.

On our website you will find other interesting, and possibly different walks around the British Isles, which are equally as picturesque and enjoyable as the ones in this book.

Should you wish to comment on this book or give further information to help keep the book updated then please write to the address below or e-mail via the website. An acknowledgement will be given:-

Challenge Publications
7, Earlsmere Drive,
Ardsley
Barnsley
S71 5HH

Notes: